Motherpeace
Tarot Guidebook

Motherpeace

Tarot Guidebook

Karen Vogel

U.S. GAMES SYSTEMS, INC.
Publishers
Stamford, CT 06902

Library of Congress Catalog Card Number: 94-060546

ISBN 0-88079-747-9

10 9 8 7 6 5 4 3 2 1

Printed in Canada

U.S. Games Systems, Inc.
179 Ludlow Street
Stamford, CT 06902 USA

Contents

Dedicated to the Goddess in her many forms and manifestations. My feelings and understanding of the Goddess evolve over time and I'm strengthened and nourished by the relationship I have with Her. I also dedicate this book to my community who love and watch over me and to all of those who love and watch over the earth.

Acknowledgements

Many friends, family and colleagues have helped with the original creation and publication of the Motherpeace deck and I thank them all. Lily Hillwomyn is the artist who did the calligraphy and painted the original drawings with me. Cassandra Light gave us the name Motherpeace and is the artist of the back design. Hillary Hurst and Sioux Jones both helped in important ways when the cards were first published.

A number of people helped with suggestions and ideas. Z. Budapest generously shared her wisdom, which among other things led to my uncrossing the legs of the women in the Two of Cups. This is an important change for a card that is about opening to love. I also thank Betsy Ferber for suggesting to us that the woman in the original drawing of the 0 Fool should be the XXI World card.

I'm of course grateful to Vicki Noble who co-created the deck with me. Although we have since gone on our separate creative paths, we continue as part of each other's extended families and share in a broader community that includes the more than 150,000 people who have the Motherpeace deck. Many people have thanked me for the deck and I'm honored by their gratitude and support. I also thank my mother and father for their appreciation of the deck.

Through the editing process, Jennifer Berezan's skillful eye helped parts of the book take form. Deborah Matthews gave wise council to me at critical points in the book's development.

Most of all I'm grateful to Nonnie Welch who generously offered to edit and provide her opinions, as well as give me a place to work through my ideas. Nonnie dusted off my mind and heart to write this book and to reach beyond where I could have gone on my own.

Introduction

My first experience with the tarot was when I was a teenager in New York City in the late 1960's. A friend offered to do a reading for me, and I remember feeling both frightened and excited. I was amazed that the reading revealed such true things about my life, and I knew there was something special about the tarot cards. Yet I also remember feeling as if I had been dropped into a foreign country where I didn't understand the language.

Shortly after that I went into my first spiritual bookstore. Again I felt an exhilaration mixed with fear as I bought my first tarot deck and book, but when I tried to use them I didn't get anywhere with the cards and I found the book unreadable. I put both the deck and book away.

Ten years later I was living in the Bay Area in California. It was the late 1970's, and tarot and other subjects such as astrology, alternative healing, psychic phenomena, and the Goddess were exploding all around me. I was again exposed to the tarot, but this time a wealth of people and books were all around me, helping me to understand the language.

During this time, I was partners in research and writing with Vicki Noble. My academic foundation was in anthropology and biology, Vicki's degree was in women's studies. We wanted to find the root of the subjugation of women, which seemed to be connected to a repression and control of sexuality and spirituality. We used our scholarly training and applied ourselves to psychic studies and Goddess history. The tarot became a large part of what we researched and experienced.

One of the big rules I learned in science is to always remain objective and be an outside observer. I had to alter that perspective because studying the tarot for me involved using the cards and doing readings, very subjective activities. I developed a passionate relationship with the cards and immersed myself in doing readings for myself and for many friends. Within a year of beginning to really use the cards, I was drawing the Motherpeace deck with Vicki.

At first Vicki thought she would do the deck alone but I was so inspired by the idea that I experimented with a drawing of the Chariot, and it was obvious to both of us that the deck was the vehicle for our research and creative partnership. The Chariot was a drawing of a woman on a journey. She seemed to say she could complete whatever she took on. As it turned out, when Vicki slowed down toward the end of our designing the deck, I completed the research and drawing of the remaining cards.

I took over publishing the deck, and Vicki went on to write *Motherpeace: A Way to the Goddess Through Myth, Art and Tarot*. Vicki's fire began the deck with the Six of Wands—a woman on fire. In the end I used the quiet determination of my first card, the Chariot, to carry the deck through to the end.

Self-publishing was a whole new territory which took me out of the realm of scholar and artist and into the world of business. I simultaneously learned how to start a business, direct the manufacturing process of a new product, and prepare the cards for printing.

Once the Motherpeace deck was printed, I had the equally daunting job of distributing and promoting the tarot deck. Also, the cards had to be hand collated and packaged. By the end of the first edition I had dealt, boxed and delivered 5000 decks. Now those first decks have taken root in people's lives and sown the seeds for 150,000 more decks.

The Motherpeace Tarot gave me a reason to learn how to be a business entrepreneur. The livelihood provided by the business has given me time to create art, particularly the slow art of wood carving and beading. I was also free to leave the city and live a life closer to nature. The wild lands of Arizona and northern California, where I have lived for many years, have been my main source of creative inspiration and wisdom.

I began this book when I realized that I had my own particular slant on the meanings of the cards. My perspective comes from my original research when I drew the cards, and my subsequent fourteen years of experience since I published the deck. I hope what I have written will make it easier to use the cards, and that the Motherpeace Tarot will help in fine-tuning your ability to guide your own life.

Karen Vogel
Point Reyes, CA
August, 1995

"Don't let anyone tell you—
you can't have empathy with your subject
and be objective."
—Jane Goodall

Tarot History

Tarot card imagery will make more sense if you know something about the historical perspective and artistic style used by the people behind a particular deck. Tarot imagery originally developed in the Middle Ages in Europe. Many of the tarot decks available today use imagery from that period in European history and come from a predominantly male perspective. The Rider-Waite deck is the most widely known example of medieval-style imagery. Other decks draw from different historical periods and geographic areas. Another widely used deck is the Thoth Deck by Aleister Crowley. He primarily used ancient Egyptian and Celtic inspiration for his designs.

No one knows exactly how tarot cards originated. Playing cards first appeared in the 1300's in medieval Europe. The earliest full-fledged tarot deck dates back to the 1400's in Renaissance Italy. Playing cards and tarot cards share a common history: the four suits in playing cards correspond to the Minor Arcana, or four suits in the tarot deck. The joker in playing cards is thought to stand for all the twenty-two Major Arcana in the tarot. Playing cards can be used in the same way as the tarot for divination, although they are more familiar as tools for gambling and other games. The virtue or wisdom in the cards has been hidden by a vice or game.

I've come to believe that a lot of wisdom was incorporated in the tarot. I feel, as do others, that ancient keepers of the old ways or earth-based spirituality wanted to pass on information. As warfare increasingly became a way of life in the Dark Ages of Europe, old ways were lost as whole cities and civilizations were wiped out. It was more and more difficult to pass on oral and written traditions since whole cultures were destroyed and ancient libraries burned.

One of the traditional stories about the origins of the tarot is that the wisdom keepers in these cultures were the storytellers, artists and healers. They chose between writing a spiritual or philosophical text or putting their knowledge into a game. They decided that a game in the form of cards would last longer, be more accessible to everyone, and easier to hide.

This theory of wise ones passing on information through a game is a compelling one for me, whether or not it is historically true. Regardless of how exactly the tarot came into being, the messages encoded in the cards themselves reflect the morality and world views of an earlier time. For me, the tarot is a bridge back into an era when people lived in communities that supported an individual's uniqueness as well as the welfare of the group as a whole.

In these earlier times it seems that a high value was placed on artistic expression and ritual. One important indication of that is the huge number and variety of Goddess figurines that are found all over the world. Perhaps each person had their own Goddess image through which they had a personal and direct relationship with the divine. I call this period of time Goddess history.

Of course the Goddess is many things to many people. Perhaps our ancestors thought of each of their individual figurines as being part of a greater whole or Great Mother archetype, who was a universal deity. There may also have been many different regional Goddesses. These local deities may have represented different attributes, such as a death Goddess or corn Goddess, with each culture having a whole pantheon of Goddesses relating to a variety of aspects of life.

The Motherpeace Tarot deck images are gathered from ancient Goddess cultures and other earth-based people, because Vicki and I realized that those cultures were perhaps an original and more direct source for the wisdom we found in the tarot. We incorporated images of people in a variety of roles focusing on times and places where women were leaders or active participants in spheres beyond their immediate families. The Motherpeace cards became more than a divination tool for us; they were, and are, a fundamental healing process for reaching beyond the limitations of the gender roles found in our society.

If you want to understand our deck, it will help to have a look at the Goddess history we use in the cards.

Goddess History

History is often written on thin ice. Think about your own family history and how much a story can change depending on who tells it. Sometimes a lot of details and events can be left out in someone's recollection. Our knowledge of history is very incomplete, especially when we go far back in time; if you go far enough back there are no written records or large cities to dig up. We rely on only a small amount of information to piece together the story of a culture.

Thirty thousand years ago, our ancestors left behind stone tools and some of the most extraordinary art anyone has ever created. It might be expected that since women comprise about half the human population, they might make up half the human images. But in many times and places, particularly in the ancient art, female imagery predominated.

There was incredible scope and variety in the images. The mind of the artist has no limits and this is nowhere more evident than the many ways the female is depicted. The images are called a variety of names: Goddesses, priestesses, and female figurines are the most common terms used to describe them.

Of course we may never know exactly what the people of these cultures of the past actually thought about the subjects of their work. But the images, taken as a whole, always seem like Goddesses to me. My conclusion is supported by many other people's work, including the extensive research of archaeologist Marija Gimbutas. At least for now, we have to be content with a great deal of speculation and guesswork about what the art actually meant to the people who created it.

Vicki and I went through a huge amount of material in our studies. We gathered many images and information from art books on the subject of Prehistoric and Primitive Art. We were struck by the abundance of female imagery from all over the world; it ranged in time from when art was first made, 30,000 or more years ago, right up through the present.

We decided, as have other feminist scholars, that it was essential to put women as well as indigenous people back into the human story. History is a much bigger story than who won various wars. There is no evidence of war before 10,000 years ago.

For a long time, many parts of the world were untouched by any systematic warfare or mass killings of whole cultures. In Europe, peaceful Goddess civilizations date back almost 10,000 years (see bibliography for Marija Gimbutas's work on Old Europe in 6500-3500 BC).

Europe began to shift toward more volatility and war about 5,000 years ago. As warfare developed and spread in various places, some people fled and some fought back. In ancient Greek history and art from 2,500 years ago, there are stories of Amazons or women warriors who fought against the Greeks.

The people who fled wars probably dispersed wherever they could. In some parts of the world, including Europe, there were places wilder or farther away from the centers of war that remained relatively uncolonized up until the times of the Renaissance. Some people may have gone to the Americas. The most convincing evidence I've seen relating to this theory are clay heads found in Mexico between 1660 BC and 300 AD. The people look African, Asian and European, which means these groups probably knew about each other. How? At this point we can only guess.

Drawings by Laurelin Remington-Wolf

Terracotta heads from Mexico 660 B.C.–300 A.D.

There are scholars who believe there were frequent and widespread pre-1492 (Columbus landing in the Americas) voyages between all the continents. Maybe there was widespread trade and cultural exchange, or perhaps it was only freak storms shipwrecking people from far-away places on the shores of the Americas. Whatever the actual story we do have these clay heads to remind us that people in Mexico possessed some knowledge about African, Asian and European people more than 2,000 years ago.

By the Renaissance, Christianity had dominated Europe as both a political and religious power. Women who were often the healers and spiritual leaders in their communities were the primary targets during Inquisition in which as many as 9 million people died. Those who threatened church authority or knew about ritual and healing went underground or were killed and their land seized. Certain information went with the people into hiding and became secret. It was in this atmosphere that tarot began and subsequently spread all over Europe, and eventually the world.

The Motherpeace deck is rooted in the tradition of the tarot but reaches farther back into a pre-patriarchal world where the Goddess flourished, people lived in peace, and nature was revered. To our present-day mind it may seem like a romantic "golden age" that never existed except in a mythological sense. Yet these Goddess civilizations have been excavated and show no evidence of fortification, which is proof that the people lived without war. By understanding what might have worked in the past, I believe it is possible to realign our present day lives with age-old practices that provided for everyone's basic needs and encouraged peace.

$\mathcal{T}$he $\mathcal{M}$otherpeace $\mathcal{T}$arot

The Motherpeace Tarot deck is made up of the traditional number of 78 cards: 22 Major Arcana and 56 Minor Arcana. The Minor Arcana are divided into four suits:

Wands (fire, energy)

Cups (water, emotions)

Swords (air, thinking)

Discs (earth, physicality)

Each of the suits uses images from particular cultures and historical periods.

The suit of Wands we located in ancient Africa. Wands represent fire. The use of fire takes use back to our human origins. It's generally accepted that humans began in Africa. These ancestors were gatherers and hunters and very well may have lived in mother-centered groups (see Tanner and Zihlman in the bibliography). We think these mother-centered groups existed before humans consciously had a concept of a deity. These first groups probably developed into the earliest Goddess cultures.

The suit of Cups relates to water, and is thus located around the Mediterranean Sea during the transition from the full-blown Goddess cultures more than 5,000 years ago to the early patriarchal cultures. We used images primarily

8

from Crete and Greece, as these cultures developed around the sea.

The Ten of Cups and Daughter of Cups are set in the Southwest United States. There is a connection between the Southwest and ancient Crete if only in the artist's imagination. An example is that the Hopi of the southwest United States and the people of Crete used the same labyrinth design. The Moon card of the Major Arcana has this design in the foreground. Perhaps they came up with this design independently and share a spiritual resonance. Or perhaps Hopi and Cretan people had actual contact and exchange of designs and culture some time in the past.

The suit of Swords uses images from a time when domination by war became a way of life in many parts of Europe. Swords are about air. We strike a cautionary note with our use of war-based cultures in our images, because when thinking and mental processes are cut off from emotions, consequences, or the earth, the results are usually destructive. We particularly used images from Greece, as it is often viewed as the birth place of European civilization and so-called rational thinking.

The suit of Discs symbolizes earth energy, which is deeply embodied by indigenous people of the Americas and by European folk and Goddess traditions. The folk or pagan traditions of Europe survived in secret or in folk art, including the tarot, despite the Inquisition with its torture and burning of witches for 500 years. Indigenous people of the Americas have also kept traditions alive during 500 years of conquest, colonization and attempts at Christianization. These earth-based traditions are still with us through teachings and traditions that have been passed on from generation to generation, and also received directly from the earth.

The Major Arcana images are from all over the world and range in time from a modern-day fantasy in the XIX Sun card to art from 30,000 years ago. In the Major Arcana we use all the cultures and geographic areas found in the four Suits or Minor Arcana. We mixed information and artifacts in many of the cards in a way that isn't strictly accurate to archeology, since on occasion we put something dug up in Europe in the hands of a woman from Africa. The cards are not meant to be actual reconstructions of modern-day people or past cultures or historical events. Instead they are imagined worlds which can be entered like universal dreams for the purposes of gathering knowledge from a variety of cultures and from the earth herself.

How to Use the Tarot

The cards are a useful tool for self-reflection. They help to bring information from the deep intuitive and creative parts of ourselves and create a dialogue between our internal and external lives. I also feel that through the tarot we can have a conversation with the Goddess or some wise and caring part of the spirit world to give us the insight and guidance we need to understand what's going on in our lives.

The Goddess is for me a multi-layered experience. At the outer limits of my ability to comprehend anything is the Great Mysterious or void, out of which comes the Creator. The Creator is female and gives birth to everything else. This Great Mother or Goddess has many different aspects or expressions in my life. Sometimes I may call on the ancient Greek Goddess Artemis to bring me strength so I can be a capable and independent woman. Or I might create an altar to Oshun, a Yoruba goddess from Africa, to help me love and see the beauty in myself. When I do a tarot reading I call on one or all of the Goddesses to be with me as witnesses and guides.

The tarot can be used for divination or to look into the future by showing what is likely to occur if certain trends or stories play themselves out. Depending on how skillfully the cards are interpreted, we can become like oracles giving prophecy or providing wise council. Divination or looking to an oracle to tell the future is a tricky business because there is a tendency to turn too much power over to the oracle, especially if the cards and the person doing the reading have proven accurate in the past.

Fortunately the cards seem to have a way of giving useless or confused responses if we become too dependent on them. We are forced to put aside the tarot and live our lives, without being intent on knowing what's going to happen in the future or over-processing and over-analyzing the paths we take. A reading should be more than a way of showing off a skill at reading someone's life and telling them what to do. It's important to be a responsible tarot reader who gives an honest reading that is truly helpful and designed to strengthen someone's inner purpose.

If you are new to the tarot it may seem as if you have entered into a mysterious and awesome place. The tarot could even be something that you can't relate to. It is best to start simple. I became familiar with the tarot by picking a card for the day and seeing if anything in particular in the picture caught my eye, perhaps also reading the meanings for the card to see what made sense. I'd take what I'd gotten from the image and meaning and then pay attention to the actual quality of the day to see what that teaches me about the meaning of the card. I built up a more complete relationship with each card over time.

Before I pick up my deck, I create a sacred space and focus my energy, which may include some form of meditation or centering activity; perhaps I'll breathe deeply or take care of myself in some other way I might need. I may light a candle or burn incense to clean out my environment of anything that might get in the way of my attention and access to information. My routine before I get out the cards depends on where I am and how much time I have to prepare myself for the reading. I've found that the more I use the cards, the easier it is to create sacred space and focus on my question without a lot of preparation.

I have a particular place or cloth on which I use the cards, and I keep my deck in a special bag or container. It's important to me that the tarot cards live in a beautiful home, though I'm not always formal about where I do a reading since I might be someplace without my divination cloth or table and still want to use the cards.

Sometimes I ask simple questions in which I pick only one card, or I may have a more complex or general question with many interrelated parts and then I'll do a whole reading. A simple question might ask: what would it look like if I took a particular course of action? Then I might ask: what would it look like if I *didn't* take that action? If I have several options available, I would pick a card for every option and see what each had to offer. I can use this one-card reading to focus on aspects of my life such as work, close relationships, or my creative and spiritual life.

One question may lead to another or to a need for clarification if an answer seems confusing or not to make sense. I may also ask for helper cards if I've picked something that indicates some difficulty or a stress point. I'll ask for help on how to rectify or learn from a situation that I want to be different. I will consciously pick another card to replace the one I want to change. I don't consider that to be cheating or somehow overriding the oracle because I'm aware of the unwanted card but know I have the choice to bring something more useful into my life by picking a different one.

Before I pick a card, I shuffle while focusing on the question which may change or become clear while I'm shuffling. As I shuffle the cards I think about what I'm asking and make sure that I'm open to getting an answer that might be different from what I want. At some point in the shuffling the cards will feel done to me. It's a kind of faith or knowing that comes through my hands when I'm handling the cards. I trust myself to know that moment when the cards are "cooked" or done being shuffled. Finally, I call upon the Goddess or whatever I hold sacred to help me be clear, truthful, and healing in my reading.

I pick a card by cutting the deck and selecting the card at the bottom of the pile I just took off the deck. I use my left hand for cutting because I feel that it has a more direct line to the intuitive right side of my brain and the Goddess or my spiritual source. I don't think there is a right way to use the tarot, although I do think it helps to develop your own rituals. There are many ways of giving respect to the relationship with your deck. Some people don't want their deck touched by anyone else; on the other hand, I don't mind if my deck is handled by someone I trust.

When I pick a card I use it like a dream image which may at times become as real as a vivid dream, as if I've entered into a card and it becomes alive in my life in some way. I've also had characters from the cards show up in my dreams, which enriches my understanding of the images.

A *Full Layout*

To begin a reading, decide how to ask the question in a way that the cards can respond with a helpful answer. I can't just turn my life over to the cards and ask, "What should I do?" A better way to formulate the question might be to ask for a picture or story of how would it be if I took a particular action or what do I have to learn from a particular situation.

I have often turned to the cards for understanding dynamics in a relationship whether it's personal or work-related. I will ask about myself in relation to someone else, or them in relation to me, or perhaps for a reading on the nature of the relationship. I can use this information to improve communication and create positive interactions. I don't do this kind of reading in order to have an edge or inside track on someone so I can then manipulate them or try and coerce them into a particular action. I find that using power over someone invariably backfires and has much worse consequences than whatever short-term benefit I may have gained.

I may want to do a general reading to give an overall picture at a particular time in my life, and I don't have to be any more specific than that. There are times in my life when I have a lot of questions or need to ask the same one more than once. Eventually I may get readings that make no sense and then I know it's time to put the cards away for now. The tarot has an uncanny way of knowing when I'm serious and in need of help or just obsessed.

When the cards are shuffled I cut the deck. My particular ritual is to use my left hand and cut twice to the left so the deck is in three piles. Then I stack them back up into one pile, picking up from right to left. Now I'm ready to lay the cards out for the reading. I lay the whole reading out and then consider the cards one at a time in the order I put them down.

A reading tells a story as I go from place to place in the following layout and piece it together in response to my question. I don't have to take the whole reading in all at once; instead, I go step-by-step through to the end, gradually building the pattern as I go through all the cards. Sometimes I can see the whole pattern or story instantly when I lay the cards out, and I'll pay attention to those first overall impressions and see what jumps out at me. There may be some interesting relationships between the cards in which a character in one card will seem to be aiming energy or turning away from a character in another card. That interaction can be woven into the story and will provide additional hints in putting together the puzzle or overall thread of a reading.

1. **Significator** is the starting point of who or what I am right now at the time of the reading.
2. **Atmosphere** is the event, catalyst or action that sets the stage for the reading and is what's behind the reading or question I'm asking.
3. **Crosscurrent** is the lesson I'm learning which may tell me about a skill that I need to acquire.

4. **Root** is what I'm standing on or the unconscious influences and what I feel in my body.

5. **Passing Away** is an event in the recent past, such as last week or even earlier in the day and it is important to the reading in some way.

6. **Sky** is what hangs over the reading. It is my head, conscious self, or spirit connection, and sometimes represents my personality or how I act in the world.

7. **Near Future** is an event that will happen soon, probably in the next week or as soon as later in the day and is something that is significant to the overall reading.

8. **Self-Concept** is how I feel or think about myself and I pay attention to whether it is in harmony or conflict with the Significator. The Self-Concept is an attitude and it can be changed or updated if it seems to lag behind what the rest of the reading is saying about me.

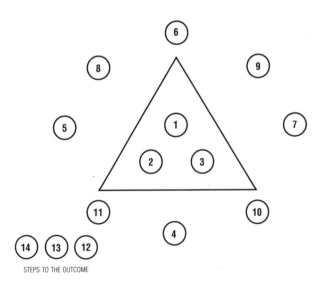

STEPS TO THE OUTCOME

9. **Hopes and Fears** could be either or both a hope and a fear. If the card is a Major Arcana, it is a current reality as well.

10. **House** is an individual or group that is important to the reading in some way and may be a source of support or a negative influence. If I've asked a question about myself in relation to someone I read the card as the person I've asked about otherwise see who I think the card is in relation to the question.

11. **Outcome**–If the card is a Major Arcana it indicates how the reading or cycle will turn out or resolve itself. If the card is a Minor Arcana or suit you can turn over until you get a Major Arcana up to three more cards, whichever happens first. The Minor Arcana are then read as "steps to the outcome" which is more distant and if there is no Major Arcana pay less attention to the four Minor Arcana and know that the outcome is yet to be determined. I take no outcome to mean that I'm not far enough along in the story or I don't have enough pieces of the puzzle to put it together and see the whole picture.

When I've looked at each card in turn, I'll see if certain numbers or suits predominate and I'll notice the number of Major Arcana to see if I get any other hints about a pattern or trend that feeds into the overall reading. I may leave the reading out for future reference or I may see if there are a few cards in particular that I want to put on an altar or somewhere that I will notice them to remind me of a particular energy I want to bring into my life. Afterwards, I give thanks for the help I've received.

$\mathcal{M}$otherpeace $\mathcal{M}$eanings

The following meanings of each card are meant to be guide posts or jumping-off points for your own journey. You will have your own unique experience of each card so don't let the written meanings overpower your own intuition and experience. Likewise, don't let your attachment to a certain outcome block seeing what the card is saying to you. There is a tendency to rewrite meanings to suit a desired outcome. It requires openness and love with yourself and others to do an honest reading. The things that are hard to see, say or hear can often be places for growth and insight.

The interpretations will help you to develop your own critical thinking about situations in your life, especially if you are stuck in an illusion, fantasy or destructive pattern. The meanings may help you to see where you are off track. When you read yourself and those close to you, you can consistently check your interpretations of the cards by what actually happens over time.

The Motherpeace deck is round. This means that the cards spin naturally as you shuffle. When a card is turned over it can appear at any angle. I have reduced the meanings to four positions for each card: Upright, left, right and reversed. If a card lands in between, read the meaning on either side, to get a sense of the in-between meaning. You can rely most on the meaning that is closest to the position the card is turned. With time and experience, you will develop a sense of how the in between positions are interpreted.

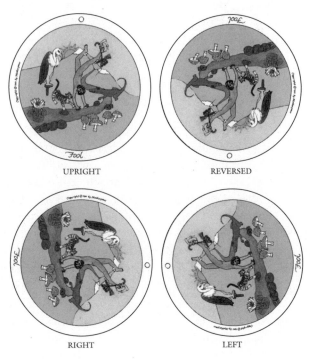

UPRIGHT   REVERSED

RIGHT   LEFT

You can also read all the positions in order to understand how a card changes as it turns.

Feel free to switch around the gender I use in the meanings to suit the gender of the person you are reading or the different parts inside yourself. You may find yourself drawn to a particular aspect of a card which has a special meaning to you. Let the animals, plants, people and other elements in the Motherpeace Tarot cards speak to different parts of your psyche.

$\mathcal{M}$ajor Arcana

The Major Arcana are the twenty-two Roman-numeral cards in the Motherpeace deck. They represent energy that is outside our personalities or outside our control. The cards carry the weight of the deep cyclical forces in nature; they may come into our lives like gentle summer rains if it's the Star card, or hit like a bolt of lightning if it's the Tower. Major Arcana are visual attempts to represent patterns from the Great Mysterious or the void.

When a Major Arcana comes up in a reading, pay attention to the particular kind of energy that is present or absent in the card. The Major Arcana speak most directly to the soul or spirit side of ourselves.

0 Fool

The Fool is off on an adventure. She wants to cross the river walking on her hands. The cat is testing the water to make sure it's not too deep to cross. The Fool wants to see the *aminita muscara* mushrooms on the other side. The mushrooms are deadly if approached incorrectly.

The pygmy crocodile already warned the Fool of possible dangers.

The Fool's only possession is a bag of truth painted with an open eye. She rings the bells and shakes the peacock feather to call in the Goddess. The Goddess comes as a griffon-vulture to bless the journey at the beginning of a new day.

UPRIGHT The Fool lives in a world where everything is possible. She is the Goddess's special and favorite child. The Fool is a sacred clown who breaks social convention, opens hearts and stands closest to the spirit. She represents the pure impulse to act and create no matter what anyone says. This energy reminds us to be awake and open to possibilities at each moment.

LEFT It may be hard to follow playful impulses or deep desires now. Pay attention to what happens with Fool energy. Does the Fool feel shy or overly serious?

RIGHT For one reason or another, a lot of effort is made to be spontaneous, have a good time or relax.

REVERSED The Fool fears looking foolish; perhaps she fears failure or some other disappointment, or the consequences of taking some risk or action. She worries about the future.

I *Magician*

The Magician is performing a ritual. She puts on her leopard robe as a commitment to the pursuit of justice. She takes up the knife as a tool to conduct the lightning of the mind through her heart. In her heart she transforms the lightning into the creative fire of the torch.

The Magician begins the ritual by looking to the Goddess of Wisdom who lives in the Egyptian Sphinx. She asks the Sphinx to watch her dance in the full spotlight of the sun. She lifts one foot and fills a beautiful cup with all the water she desires. From her other foot pours seeds and whatever else she needs to build her ritual toward its end.

UPRIGHT The Magician takes action. The creative impulse of the Fool is brought into form. She has the ability to get things done with focused energy and power. The Magician represents outward fiery energy. She is able to harness all the elements to get the desired results.

LEFT The energy or will of the Magician is held back or hard to access. There is a lack of confidence.

RIGHT The Magician is using a lot of effort and pushing hard to make something happen.

REVERSED The Magician's potential is unable to come out right now. Self-doubt is preventing the expression of her power or individuality. If this energy is too long repressed or reversed, there is a tendency to abuse power. The Magician may hurt someone and/or herself.

II *High Priestess*

The High Priestess sits down to wait for a meeting with the Goddess. The Goddess comes after the High Priestess cleanses herself by shedding her menstrual blood.

The Goddess asks the High Priestess to be a guardian at the gateway. The High Priestess accepts the responsibility of sitting with open arms at the doorway of life and death. The gateway is made up of two pillars. The pillar on the left is the owl Goddess in an abstract form. The owl has distilled knowledge from her life's experiences. On the right is a pillar with a geometric design symbolizing what remains to be done and what lies ahead.

UPRIGHT   The High Priestess sits at the gate way of wisdom. She is the doorway to inner knowledge, and an affirmation of being true to a path, destiny or purpose in life. She's sanctified. The High Priestess is receptive and open at the doorway to the intuitive psychic realm. She points inside for the answers.

LEFT   The High Priestess feels uncertain. She disbelieves her insights or has partial understanding right now.

RIGHT   The High Priestess is trying to stay connected to her unconscious or inner world. Perhaps she seeks ways to tap into her dreams and inspirations.

REVERSED   It's difficult for the High Priestess to access her inner world. She's having a hard time trusting her judgment. She can't see below the surface and needs meditation or some other tool to reconnect with her inner wisdom.

Note: In both the High Priestess and the Temperance cards, I've used images of women of the Ngere tribe from the Ivory Coast. After the deck was published I found out that the costumes, body painting and dancing of these women comes from a ritual done after cliterodectomies. It seems a contradiction to have the power of the High Priestess and Temperance cards framed in a ritual that includes female genital mutilation, which is an extreme and brutal repression of female sexuality and a violation of fundamental human rights.   Still I am inspired by the extraordinary dance, music and regalia, which I hope will live on in powerful rituals without female genital mutilation. Efua Dorkenoo, a leader in women's health, says, "What is needed is group activities which help women lay to rest old rituals of passage which prepared them to fit into male dominated societies and to discover new forms of initiation which prepare them for life in the 1990's and beyond."

III *Empress*

The Empress is relaxing. It's a warm summer day and she savors the fruits of past work. Covered with nothing more than a leopard skin blanket, she smells a rose and enjoys a peaceful moment. She knows that the earth is bountiful because she has worked to make it so. A bull stands at a distance, alert and ready to bring in the harvest when the Empress needs his help.

The Empress has positioned herself in a circle of her favorite ancestors.

In the foreground is the Greek mother Goddess Demeter. She holds harvested grain in her hands, with snakes wrapped around her arms.

Behind Demeter sits a large mother Goddess between two leopards. She comes from the ancient city of Catal Hüyük in Turkey. Catal Hüyük is an important early Goddess city where the people lived in peace for more than a thousand years.

In back of the Empress's head is the Great Mother of Laussel carved at the entrance of a cave in France 30,000 years ago.

The Empress stops long enough to look in the mirror, enjoy a visit with her friends and plan her next move.

UPRIGHT The Empress is the Earth Mother in all the abundant diversity and physicality of nature. She is active and receptive depending on what is required. There is a grace and finesse in her action. She is charismatic and able to handle a great deal.

LEFT The Empress is uneasy in her life or body. She can't find a channel or form for expressing her creativity or sexuality.

RIGHT The Empress is going after something. Her creative expression requires some struggle or concentrated attention.

REVERSED The Empress is in a period of dormancy. She may feel as if she can't take care of herself or anyone else. The Empress may feel that her creativity is dried up. It's winter, a cyclical period of rest.

IV *Emperor*

Here is a picture of what happens when the Emperor grows up without having developed a sense of community responsibility and respect for the earth. This card is a portrait of Alexander the Great, a man who wanted to rule the world.

Love would connect him if only he could uncross his arms and let it in. Instead he dulls his senses by the over-consumption of his spoils from war.

A woman is forced from her home, and her village is burned. A musician skips off into the background as if he could undo the damage done by the Emperor.

The Emperor thinks about what he wants next. He sends the Goddess away and is trapped in his own glorified image of himself.

UPRIGHT The Emperor is the wielder of raw power. He holds fast to his plans and stands his ground with an eye on expansion. This energy can be destructive if it overlooks consequences to other people or the environment. How we use this energy is critical to our quality of life. This is the energy of a four-year-old who wants to own the world and shouts "Mine!" He needs help to remind him when to share.

LEFT The Emperor's power isn't getting out. He may be unsure of himself and find it hard to take a stand or have control.

RIGHT The Emperor is using a lot of force to assert himself. He is rigid and aggressive. The Emperor may try to do things for himself while saying it's for other people's good.

REVERSED The Emperor's concept of power is overturned. He rejects domination and the abuse of power. The Emperor softens and becomes more loving. A numbness or stiffening in the Emperor's body is released.

V Hierophant

In the Motherpeace image the Hierophant has stolen his power from those around him. He is dressed up like a woman in a robe and false breasts. He is trying to disguise the underlying biases in his teaching. His scroll is blank, waiting for the next plan or book of rules.

The women are confused or forced into paying homage to his authority. In return they receive bits of wine and wafers. His systems and structures depend on people being locked away from their own sources of power.

Behind the armed guard, stained glass window and stone wall is nature. Nature is a direct source of information and authority. The Hierophant needs to know when to step aside.

UPRIGHT This is the organizer or authority in charge of rules and regulations. He is a systems maker or teacher. Sometimes the Hierophant can indicate a time for dealing with authority such as courts, school, organized religion or some hierarchal system or institution. He is the agent of conventional morality.

LEFT The Hierophant is questioning the conventional wisdom of the culture, but not yet outwardly challenging it.

RIGHT The Hierophant is actively challenging what he no longer believes.

REVERSED The Hierophant breaks free from the control of people or ideas that prevent him from following his sense of truth or personal authority. He no longer relies solely on experts or parental authority. The Hierophant is in active rebellion.

VI Lovers

A bright pink ground of self-love has flooded through the gap, sweeping aside the oppressive myths and fantasies on the Greek vases. The walls of the Emperor and the Hierophant have opened. Lovers merge in geometric shapes. Sudden energy reverberates in an ecstatic shudder through the sky and the sun sets above a rose arbor. The Lovers know all is right with the world for they are at peace.

UPRIGHT The Lovers bring people together passionately. There is a magnetic charge drawing the Lovers toward people, places or things. In this time of choice they are rushing toward their heart's desire. It's a powerful attraction of opposite poles. Sometimes this powerful attraction can be between parts of a person wanting to come together, or it is the Lovers wanting to unite with each other.

LEFT The Lovers are holding back for fear of rejection. They are not trusting their hearts. Perhaps they are not sure of their choices.

RIGHT The Lovers go after what they want. They are initiating the relationship or activity and making things happen.

REVERSED The Lovers are unable to make a choice. It's a hard time in their relationship. Perhaps there are conflicts, pain of separation, dominance issues, gender bias, or power struggles. The Lovers are called to work through conditioned fantasies about romance and partnership in order to come together.

VII *Chariot*

The woman in the chariot is an Amazon from northern Africa. The Goddess just gave her the reward of an apple for a job well done. The Amazon now has the courage to continue on her journey.

Her winged goats guide her travels without the need for her to hold the reigns and steer. The goats look up and down so they can see what's far away and close at hand. They are pulling her chariot on a path guided by her deep sense of purpose. She knows where she wants to go; at least, she trusts she's headed in the right direction.

Nut, the Egyptian Goddess, is the night sky watching over the Amazon's journey. She draws on the energy of Cancer (the crab) to create a container that is strong and safe, particularly for those times when the journey is hard.

The Amazon holds her double-headed axe for all to see. She declares to the world what she has accomplished and mastered. The Gorgon head on the side of the Chariot warns away anyone who might impede her journey. Her path is chosen.

UPRIGHT The Chariot focuses on accomplishing her goals. She uses discipline and determination to succeed or win. She knows how to move around in the world and take care of herself. She is in the driver's seat of her life.

LEFT The Chariot has some personal doubts. She is not fully behind what she is doing.

RIGHT The Chariot may be doing more than necessary. She wants to make sure she is in charge. She must be careful not to abuse power and override everyone else.

REVERSED The Chariot is knocked down or overwhelmed and she must be sure not to take it out on someone else. She might need to pick herself up and try again to make an effort to move forward and take the next step. Things are not in her control.

VIII *Justice*

The three Norse Goddesses of Destiny have stopped at the ash tree. They want to listen and respond to all of life.

A Goddess holds a crystal in one hand. Through the stone she connects down to the pulse or giant crystal at the center of the earth. Her other hand lies on the root of the tree.

At the same time, a second Goddess gives the tree water. Then she feels with her other hand to make sure that the tree is getting what it needs.

A third Goddess completes the circle around the tree. She reaches out to touch a deer and ask him what's needed. He answers for all the animals including humans.

UPRIGHT In Justice things are happening as they should. By taking care of the central purpose the Justice insures harmony, balance or rightness in all of our lives. If someone is not feeling at peace right now, perhaps they don't see the overall picture. In Justice, the Goddesses teach about cause and effect, consequences, or karma.

LEFT There is some doubt that things are going to turn out right.

RIGHT This is a time when too much personal energy might be used to bring about an outcome without regard for the consequences.

REVERSED In Justice now life feels out of balance. Perhaps a past action may have caused a seemingly unfair or unjust situation. How can Justice take care of itself?

What can Justice do to remedy how things have turned out?

IX *Crone*

Standing at the crossroads is the Greek Goddess Hekate. She stops to listen for the messages that come from deep within herself. Behind the Crone the night sky pushes aside the sun and the daytime mind. The Moon Goddess floods the sky with lunar energy and sends the nighttime mind into the deep intuition of the Crone.

At the top of the sign at the crossroads is a laughing Goddess. She's a Pre-Columbian clay statue from Veracruz, Mexico. She tells the Crone that all roads are good and to pray for right direction. One day the Crone may teach others what she's learned. By the light of the snake on her staff, the Crone will help people to find their own paths.

UPRIGHT The Crone stands at the crossroads. She aligns herself with inner wisdom through solitude and trust. She needs simplicity or quiet to make a truthful choice. The Crone's inner teacher or deep knowledge is used for guidance.

LEFT The Crone is questioning or doubting her wisdom or direction in life.

RIGHT The Crone feels a sense of urgency to know. She hurries to come to conclusions.

REVERSED The Crone is not able to see very far into herself. She may think she knows more than she currently does. She has a tendency to jump from one thing to the next without fully digesting the significance of each move. The Crone should be careful of decisions now. She may think she sees more than she does at this point. The Crone needs an outside perspective; perhaps she should wait on making crucial decisions until she is more awake to her inner guidance and wisdom.

ascendent

x Wheel of Fortune

The Wheel of Fortune indicates a time when something lifts us out of our accustomed life and drops us somewhere new. It can feel like a twist of fate because this card is about astrological influence and cyclical change.

The Wheel of Fortune spins the energy in our lives out of everyday reality onto a new horizon or place on the wheel. Each horizon is a different square or astrological sign. Check the position of the card to find the corresponding astrological sign.

The astrological sign that falls below the horizon or ascendent is the key to what the card means in a particular situation. If the card is upright, Aries is on the ascendent. An Aries person or energy will be important in the coming change, or the change will occur around the Aries time of year.

Reversed, the Wheel of Fortune can sometimes mean a delay, or timing can be off on anything that is attempted.

ARIES: *Copper figurine from Mohenjo-Daro, India, 2400-2000 B.C.*

She is a dancer bringing forth new forms to life. Her practical attitude is grounded in giving herself to the world. She lives in spontaneous action.

TAURUS: *Rock Pictograph from Sha'ib Samma in Yemen*

The Earth Mother gives birth to a human who in turn gives birth to a baby. New life brings continuation and perfect beauty to the world. The baby will need care to grow.

GEMINI: *Eye Goddess from a temple in Syria, about 3500 B.C.*

The all-seeing Eye Goddess can be in many places at once. It's no surprise she contains twins inside herself. Every part has a counterpart helping us to be open to the unexpected.

CANCER: *Clay figure from Susa (Iraq) 3rd millennium B.C.*

The Goddess focuses energy in her heart. She holds her breasts to trust and heal herself and others with love and honesty.

LEO: *Cat Goddess from Lake Maracaibo, Venezuela*

The warmth and intensity of the cat's power is tempered by a cold discernment. Everything feeds off something else in a continuous movement of love and life.

VIRGO: *Female figure from a fresco 18th Dynasty Egypt*

Now the Aries dance of spring has come full circle to fall. Precise and contained movement bring her to a change of season. Daylight will soon be shorter than the nighttime, as the Earth approaches the time of balance at the fall equinox.

LIBRA: *Aphrodite on a white goose from a Greek cup, 470 B.C.*

The goose takes Aphrodite on a flight searching for beauty in the world. The Goddess stretches out her hand, welcoming the new experiences. She wants to teach others what she learned on her journey.

SCORPIO: *Winged gorgon, Greece*

The gorgon or snake Goddess plunges down into the deep ocean and fiery inner layer of the earth. The snake leads her down past fear into a vast ecstatic energy.

SAGITTARIUS: *Sumerian eye Goddess, 3rd millennium B.C.*

In the womb of the Goddess is a third eye. She is ready to give birth to a far-reaching view of life. Her wide-reaching vision includes the world and all its needs.

CAPRICORN: *Goats flanking the Goddess as the tree of life, 6th century B.C., Turkey*

The goats feed on the tree of life which is then fertilized by their manure. No one is left out of the work of supporting life and recycling death. The Goddess is a competent leader.

AQUARIUS: *Artemis of Ephesus, last millennium B.C.*

Artemis welcomes many to her numerous breasts. She renews her energy in quiet moments. She is ready again to open her arms to others.

PISCES: *Fish Goddess*

The Goddess has danced all the way around the astrological signs to gestate in the ocean. The sea creatures enclose her in a womb filled with a myriad of emotions and impressions. To everyone outside she may seem immobilized or in trance.

XI *Strength*

The Irish fairy Goddess Brigit has come to her place of power. She's joined by twelve animals, and she makes the thirteenth. These animals know her well and trust her. She in turn feels safe enough to expose her passion for life and the earth. She holds out her ego in the shape of a small sun. With one sniff, the wolf knows where she's going next.

UPRIGHT The Strength card is the inner fire or desire that effects transformations through powerful unseen magic. She uses this energy without fear because she feels a deep connection to community and the earth. She is the archetypal free and independent woman who knows how to use the life force, chi or kundalini energy.

LEFT Strength hesitates and may feel she wants too much. She disbelieves in the unseen forces.

RIGHT Strength uses too much energy in an inappropriate way; she tries to get someone to do her bidding.

REVERSED Strength fears her power or magic. She stops herself because she might be labeled a witch or a kook, or called superstitious and irrational.

XII *Hanged One*

In her sacred cypress grove, Artemis chooses to stop everything. She hangs by a snake. She is offering herself to the Goddess and praying. The snake joins her prayer by taking its tail into its mouth.

She waits with her hands in the river. When she finally knows why she is here, a radiant light surrounds her head. She feels whole again.

UPRIGHT The Hanged One suspends her activity or surrenders to what is. She may feel an ecstatic release or as if she is eternally waiting. She has a chance to integrate the small scope of her personality with her heart or spirit and experience a sense of inner purpose or unconditional love.

LEFT The Hanged One is ambivalent about slowing down or giving in to her inner world.

RIGHT The Hanged One keeps busy and takes on activity and, as a result, may keep away from herself.

REVERSED The Hanged One has a tendency to become involved in outside activity in order to avoid inner work. Once she is in this pattern, it may take time for her to slow down and allow the transformation to happen.

XIII *Death*

The Death Goddess places bones at the base of a birch tree. Carefully she puts the body in the shape of a fetus in a womb. Soon she will be ready for new life. The old one is over. Leaves fall to cover the bones.

A copperhead snake arrives to shed its skin. The snake turns around to watch itself change. There is still some shedding left, even though the old body is already dead.

UPRIGHT In Death, she lets go of a core part of herself. She sheds a skin, and there is usually some effort involved. She may be quite ready to make the change, but there can still be grief, anger and pain. Usually the Death refers to the ego, an attitude, or a relationship. It is about an organic and final change, but it is rarely about physical death.

LEFT She wants to slow down the process of Death and may be unsure of what is happening.

RIGHT She is impatient or struggling to get out of the old skin.

REVERSED Death is slow or unconscious. She holds onto a dead form and may not be ready to let go. She may feel numb or stuck.

XIV Temperance

The Goddess has entered the dancer's body. Her dance has set the waves of the ocean on fire. Nothing is impossible. An aurora borealis shimmers colored light across the night sky.

The wildness of the night enters her body to heal and regenerate old wounds. Her art now is everything.

UPRIGHT Temperance has learned how to direct the potential around her to a coherent purpose. She has discipline or a victory in the emotional, psychic and creative fields. She knows about the place where art and science meet and has a mastery or equilibrium in the midst of a lot of creative energy. She can be about a sexual/spiritual union and this merging feels in some way blessed by the Goddess or Great Mysterious.

LEFT For Temperance, integration is not yet possible as there are a few more steps to go through.

RIGHT Temperance uses a great deal of energy to keep herself in balance. She might be doing too much.

REVERSED Right now Temperance is fragmented. This is a necessary time of chaos in order for the parts of herself to reassemble in a more useful form. The shedding of outworn patterns or skins in the Death card has made this new integration possible. It can take awhile to bring herself back together and use the new potential. She needs to learn how to use the power available to her.

Note: See note on page 27, High Priestess.

XV Devil

Here is an image of the Devil at his worst. He's placed himself on top of everyone. He keeps a tight grip on the chain that holds his operation together. Everyone involved is bound to their predetermined part. The Devil keeps order here by force or handing out rewards for complicity.

To use the Devil well, look at the structures in your life. Look at what is working well and what isn't. Think about what you need to hold your life together. How are you impacting all that supports you?

UPRIGHT The Devil is tied to a system or structure of his own making. His survival may seem dependent on everyone conforming to his ideas which may include hierarchy, domination, or playing by the rules. Pay attention to any ways the Devil contributes or collapses into the abuse of power. He may need to look for ways to be true to himself instead of requiring the obedience of others.

LEFT The Devil is not yet entrenched in a destructive cycle. His rigidity or abuse of power is held at a distance and he does what he can to remain true to himself.

RIGHT The Devil is in a full-blown struggle to escape the control or conditioning in the misuse of power.

REVERSED The Devil breaks free from constraints and overcomes what has kept him down. His patterns or bonds are broken, freeing his spirit from a collective shadow to be able to create a new, more useful structure.

XVI *Tower*

The Goddess is called to be with her people. She is sitting on a tower that she knows will soon crumble. She has no time to consider the danger or consequences because she is struck by lightning.

Already the world has changed. They are in the middle of a solar eclipse. The people wait below. As the lightning strikes, she has a vision. She tells the people how to get to their new home.

UPRIGHT The Tower shatters the old foundations and can feel like the rug is pulled out from under her feet. If she is like a cat, she can land feet first and unhurt, although her landing will be harder and less graceful. Nevertheless, this is a dramatic change in the core of her psyche. The change may be external and striking like lightning. She is shocked by how different she feels and there is no going back. Sometimes the Tower is a strong and sudden upwelling of life force, chi or kundalini energy in a sexual or creative way.

LEFT The Tower comes into the changes slowly or with hesitation.

RIGHT The Tower is hit hard by sudden change or fate.

REVERSED Change is slow or not disruptive. She may be unaware of what is happening and it can be a relief to have changes come more gradually.

XVII *Star*

She has stopped on her journey to bathe in the healing waters of a hot spring. A gentle rain washes her free and restores her balance.

The Pleiades or Seven Sister star cluster is behind the large Dog Star Sirius. They shine on the woman, seeding her with new life. She sinks back in gratitude as the redtail hawk circles overhead.

The Navajo Goddess Changing Woman has come to walk in beauty and find good in everything.

UPRIGHT The Star is a time of healing or a period of grace and cleansing. She can renew what has been damaged in the storm of the Tower with openness, trust, love, psychic and spiritual awareness. She may experience a sense of being with the Goddess.

LEFT The Star may not be feeling very well, or may feel disconnected from healing and the Goddess.

RIGHT The Star is working to reach out for healing.

REVERSED The Star is fearing vulnerability and may have a hard time opening herself to love and healing. Perhaps she is sick and feels negative or defeated. She needs to be aware of the healing and regeneration that is possible, and find ways of reconnecting herself with what renews her energy.

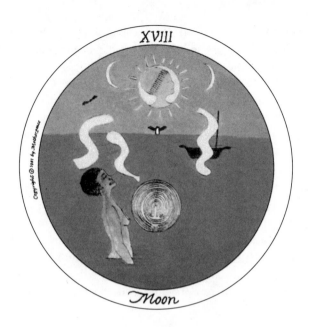

XVIII 𝓜oon

A woman is wading out into the sea to stand under the moon. Soon she will set sail in her boat. She has a dream that the Goddess will be with her on the journey through the labyrinth.

At the far end of the sea is something not quite real. Sometimes the woman thinks it's a whale's tail disappearing on the horizon. Other times she sees a winged door pointing the way out of the labyrinth.

The bat has come to speed her journey.

UPRIGHT The Moon is a strong calling or pull from deep within. Her inner purpose or spirit is taking her on a journey. The transformation or initiation is happening in a way that may be unfamiliar, taking her to an unknown outcome. She must trust herself, and her dream images may be very strong now. She may be exploring new territory in her psyche and in the unfathomable Great Mysterious.

LEFT The Moon may have doubts about the path. She may be in an early or particularly mysterious phase of inner work.

RIGHT Her mind is working overtime to comprehend what is emerging from inside her.

REVERSED If the Moon has stayed in the dark or unknown long enough, she is now coming into consciousness with something of use. Or she may be blocking the flow of information and energy from her intuition by trying to understand things too soon. She should look to her feelings and intuition and let the Goddess work in her life.

XIX Sun

People have come to party with the other animals. The circus troupe entertains the others. They are celebrating a renewal. Everyone came through the *sipápuni*, the Hopi word for the place of emergence, alive and joyous. No one is left out. There is warmth and love enough for all.

UPRIGHT The Sun is reborn after the journey or transformation of the Moon. There is happiness and understanding. Everyone knows why they are here and there is delight in this realization. Life makes sense and there is purpose and pleasure in expressing uniqueness. They no longer mourn the death of old parts.

LEFT The Sun is not yet in the full force and there is an easing into rebirth and joy.

RIGHT The Sun may be exaggerating new-found pleasure and might feel like a child trying out a new game.

REVERSED The Sun may not believe in the happiness felt or not be fully aware of the joyful change.

xx Judgement

The Goddess is the Egyptian ankh or life force pouring rainbow light from her heart. She is the planet Venus who has come to help her sister Earth at a critical time.

The Goddess is asking for us humans to bring forth our best work. She accepts all our offerings. With these offerings the world becomes a better place in which to live.

UPRIGHT Judgement is grounded in healing and love. She is connected to the Goddess in a way that goes beyond dogma and systems. She is able to give a lot to others without depleting her energy. There is a big change; a decision is made in the best interest of all.

LEFT Judgement is unaware of the full implications of a decision or change she made.

RIGHT Judgement is actively initiating a change and bringing in healing energy.

REVERSED Judgement may be overly critical or judgemental right now. Her attitude is preventing healing energy from reaching her just when she needs to renew her energy. She may be blaming others instead of taking care of herself.

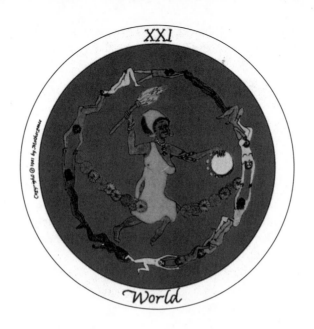

XXI *World*

The Fool has grown up into a woman of the world. Leading a spiral dance, she is followed by her circle of friends and family. She skips through a chain of peyote buttons and flowers. These sacred plants part to let her by. She's come a long way. It no longer matters to her how she looks or that her clothes are torn. She takes her place among the children of the earth.

UPRIGHT The World is breaking free into a new cycle. The old is completed and many new things are now possible since she has done her work. She knows and loves herself as all her facets have come into harmony. She may feel expanded and omnipotent because a major cycle of her life is completed and a new doorway opens.

LEFT She is moving toward a completion and there may be disbelief that the work is done, especially if it has been difficult.

RIGHT She wants to be done with the past and move on to the new life.

REVERSED The World doesn't yet realize the magnitude of ending this cycle in her life. She may be unaware of where she is, so she doesn't realize that she's completed something. She might feel like holding onto the old familiar ways for awhile longer. In time she will become comfortable and begin again as the Fool in the world where everything is possible.

ℳinor Arcana

Each of the four suits in the Minor Arcana contains fourteen cards, ace through ten and four "people" cards. The people cards are Daughter, Son, Priestess and Shaman. Each contains the energy of one of the four elements (fire, water, air and earth) plus that of the element of the suit.

Daughters - Earth
Sons - Air
Priestesses - Water
Shamans - Fire

Therefore:

Daughter of Wands is fire (Wands) and earth.
Son of Cups is water (Cups) and air.
Priestess of Swords is air (Swords) and water.
Shaman of Discs is earth (Discs) and fire.

The interplay of the two elements in the people cards is the basis for the meaning of the card.

Wands

Ace of Wands

A baby is born from a robin's blue egg and fire ignites this new life.

UPRIGHT She bursts forth with new energy or rebirth. She is in a new period of activity when fire, creativity and positive energy come out.

LEFT She has a hard time summoning enough energy to break out of her shell.

RIGHT She may feel more energy than she knows what to do with.

REVERSED She can't feel or activate her passion, fire or creativity. Perhaps she doesn't want to express anger or other strong emotions or there may be a fear of expressing active sexual energy.

Two of Wands

A woman sits and calls upon an ancestor to help her learn how to get a fire going.

UPRIGHT She knows her inner strength and sexuality, and trusts in her intuitive abilities. She feels sexual desire, or is inventive and has creative energy.

LEFT Her intuition is not fully activated.

RIGHT She may be straining to know something or activate a passion.

REVERSED She may not have the energy to get anything going and there is a tendency to feel incompetent or unable to get things done. She may feel as if her intuition is inaccessible.

Three of Wands

A mother teaches her children to express themselves creatively through art and communication.

UPRIGHT   There is a spontaneous outpouring and exchange of creative energy through communication, teaching, and learning. Parents, children, friends and community grow.

LEFT She is cautious about expressing her creative energy.

RIGHT Something is out of balance in her expression of energy. She might be trying too hard.

REVERSED A communication is blocked and she may need to speak up, even if it is difficult. Otherwise there is a chance her throat will tighten or become sore.

Four of Wands

The girls or young women are dancing to celebrate their first menstruation.

UPRIGHT She is joyously celebrating and is happily playing with others in parties or ritual.

LEFT It's hard for her to feel like letting loose or being with people in celebration right now.

RIGHT She puts out a lot of energy, perhaps to make some event happen. She needs to be sure to enjoy herself in the midst of whatever she is getting done.

REVERSED She may be working too hard and her life may be overly serious even though joy and fun may be all around. She may find her sexual energy not available.

Five of Wands

The priestesses are struggling to see who will lead as a volcano goes off in the background. The phoenix, the bird of regeneration, rises from the flames.

UPRIGHT She is struggling with others or inside herself to find the best direction to go. It is an important thrashing out of ideas and feelings.

LEFT She is hesitant about engaging in conflict.

RIGHT She is going after a confrontation.

REVERSED The lid is on whatever conflict she is having. Either it is resolved, or this is a period of temporary peace and she will have to re-engage in order to release her anger or resolve the conflict.

Six of Wands

She is a leader who has risen and taken her place on a wheel of fire.

UPRIGHT She has become a leader or winner. She experiences a burst of fire and creative energy which is like an affirmation; a big "yes."

LEFT The full force of her energy hasn't come through yet.

RIGHT She exerts a lot of power or leadership ability.

REVERSED She is not able to express her power now. Is something stopping her? Does she lack the confidence?

Seven of Wands

The priestess is challenged by her group to explain her position and defend her leadership.

UPRIGHT She takes a stand on something she firmly believes in. Her position comes from deeply held convictions or inner truths and she is willing to defend them.

LEFT She is not as willing to take a stand and may still be forming her ideas or truth.

RIGHT She is vehement about her position.

REVERSED She has a difficult time holding her ground, as anxiety, doubt and fear may be clouding her ability to stand up for herself.

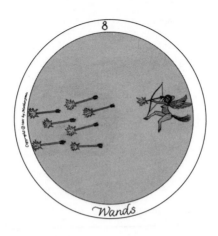

Eight of Wands

A woman, part horse and part human, is letting fly her last arrow to follow the others to the target.

UPRIGHT She has a lot of energy available and it is a good time to initiate change or aim at a specific goal.

LEFT She hesitates or is ambivalent about going in a certain direction.

RIGHT She makes a real push to get something done.

REVERSED Her energy is blocked and it may not be the right time for action. If she is afraid of taking action, she may block new awareness or energy. She may also fear the ensuing responsibility related to an action.

Nine of Wands

A wise woman sits in repose to regenerate her energy for new enterprises and action.

UPRIGHT She has wisdom and responsibility that has grown over time. She knows how to regenerate her own energy and take care of others. She has worked hard to achieve sensitivity and knowledge.

LEFT Her energy is still building back up.

RIGHT She needs to be sure to not give out more than she can handle and still have enough to be able to regenerate her own energy.

REVERSED She is run down and her energy is depleted. She needs to stop and revitalize herself.

Ten of Wands

The priestesses are having an all-night trance dance to raise energy for healing themselves and others.

UPRIGHT She has an extreme output of energy and can perhaps go too far. Has she taken on too much at once? She needs to pay attention to the effects, particularly on her nervous system.

LEFT She is using some discretion or holding back on energy.

RIGHT She has great demands on her time or energy with a tendency to over-extend herself.

REVERSED She is pulling back her energy. She may not have gone far enough or she sensed it would be a waste of her energy to continue in a particular direction.

Daughter of Wands

The Daughter is going to a new home with her companion, the unicorn. The whooping cranes guide the way.

UPRIGHT She rushes forward to a new adventure, exploding with joy in life and freedom. She's not held back by other's judgements or limitations.

LEFT She's cautious about stepping out in a new way.

RIGHT She may be heading toward recklessness or at least unusually flamboyant behavior.

REVERSED Her spontaneous energy is blocked. Is she stopping herself or letting others stop her?

Son of Wands

The Son is dressed up and performs a ritual for his community.

UPRIGHT He wants to please others and delight them with his love of life. He is an entertainer or guardian of sacred play and sexuality.

LEFT He is shy and doesn't want to look foolish.

RIGHT He exudes a great amount of energy and wants to delight others.

REVERSED He has a deep reluctance or even fear of showing his energy or sexuality. It may be a stage fright or fear of energetic public display. He is self-conscious, and stifling his clowning and playful sexual energy.

Priestess of Wands

The Priestess, with the help of the lion, just made it rain in order to renew the life and energy of her community.

UPRIGHT She has the ability to direct her creative, healing and sexual energy to bring about transformation. She is direct, passionate and loving in her action. She has a sense of purpose and the ability to go after what she wants.

LEFT She is unsure of what she is supposed to do and is not seeing a clear direction.

RIGHT She is single-minded in focusing on what's required of her.

REVERSED She finds it difficult to reach her innate power. Her enthusiasm and intuitive knowledge are suppressed, leaving her feeling frustrated or even betrayed. Perhaps fear is getting in her way, making her difficult to be around.

81

Shaman of Wands

The Shaman opens his hand to make available his power and authority to those around him.

UPRIGHT The Shaman has the ability to be strong, protective and able to handle life in all its complexity. He meets contradictions and difficulties with patience and confidence. He has the power that comes with maturity and is good at negotiation.

LEFT He lacks the energy to fully rise to the situation.

RIGHT He is given to exerting pressure to make sure things go his way.

REVERSED His problems may feel overwhelming and it's hard to see solutions. Perhaps he is withholding and doesn't want to figure out solutions, or may be afraid to try anything.

Cups

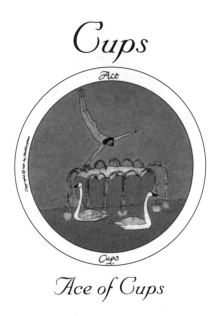

Ace of Cups

A woman dives into a cup of self-love, spilling water over onto a pair of mated swans.

UPRIGHT She loves herself. She may be falling in love with someone else and hearts are opening.

LEFT She feels a hesitation in her heart.

RIGHT She feels some extra push or expansion in her heart.

REVERSED It is hard too know how she is feeling. She can't let go into the love around her. Self-love is lacking.

Two of Cups

Two women, part fish and part human, come together in the sea. A pair of dolphins play under a crescent moon.

UPRIGHT   She has strong feelings of connection to someone or something. She is drawn toward merging or uniting or bringing together parts in herself. She creates a partnership.

LEFT   She holds back from something she desires.

RIGHT   She is following a deeply-held feeling, despite any and all obstacles.

REVERSED   She is unable to move toward someone or something. She may have fight or flight reactions and feel disconnected and lonely.

Three of Cups

Three priestesses meet at a sacred spring to create a ritual together. They are joined by an animal that is part horse, bird and fish.

UPRIGHT There is an easy and creative collaboration. She feels the positive influence of others on her life.

LEFT She feels a hesitation about completely trusting others.

RIGHT She pulls the group energy in her direction.

REVERSED She has difficulty connecting with others now. Is she afraid, especially in group situations? It may not be the time for collaboration right now. She needs to strengthen her ability to trust and relax in groups. She needs to find people (peers) that love and accept her.

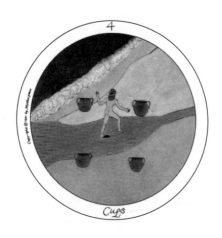

Four of Cups

A woman crosses the river at the place where it meets the ocean.

UPRIGHT She turns away from her present situation and takes time to reflect. She cleanses herself from disappointment. She's not jumping at what is offered before considering consequences.

LEFT She is, to some degree, caught up in past feelings.

RIGHT She is actively engaged in getting over some past dissatisfaction.

REVERSED She is ready to move on, and she is open to new possibilities. She has renewed her sense of hope in life and feels that opportunities await her.

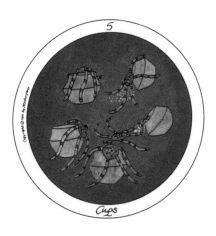

Five of Cups

The sticky starfish are tipping over the cups; some pearls have spilled out.

UPRIGHT She is grieving or letting go. There is disappointment and loss. She must not become overwhelmed, bogged down or stuck in this phase.

LEFT She may be holding off feelings of sadness or tears.

RIGHT She is actively acknowledging what has happened and how she feels about it. She needs to be sure not to cling to feeling bad or to a broken heart.

REVERSED Her feelings of hope and new possibilities are returning. She has worked through the loss and is ready to go on.

Six of Cups

Women ride horses and sea horses over the crest of a wave. They salute with a cup, out of which spirals a snake.

UPRIGHT She bursts free of emotional limitations. She feels an immediacy and intensity of emotional expression. She is transforming her life through honest expression of love or other feelings.

LEFT She isn't fully trusting herself to come out with how she feels.

RIGHT She isn't expressing great emotional intensity now.

REVERSED She can't find a way to express herself. Old wounds or memories may be in her way. She may feel unsafe or inhibited. She may have retreated or collapsed into formality and superficial interactions.

Seven of Cups

A woman is performing magic. She holds a scarf, and a dove flies out of the cup balanced on the top of her head.

UPRIGHT She is in the interior realm of dreams, wishes, and possibilities. There isn't yet a form or substance to what she imagines. This can be a relaxing and inventive time as long as she allows for being spaced out.

LEFT There is not yet clarity or cohesion in her inner world.

RIGHT She may need to plan or negotiate with others for time to be with herself.

REVERSED She has taken the time to contemplate all her fantasies, and now one thought or desire predominates. The bright plan lights up and she is pulled on a particular path. She feels inventive.

Eight of Cups

The octopus has found all her most beautiful cups.

UPRIGHT She gathers together her inner resources. She is centering on her deepest emotions or values. There are a myriad of emotions now.

LEFT She feels unstable or uncertain about her feelings.

RIGHT It's an effort for her to reach the center of her being.

REVERSED She may feel overwhelmed, swamped by emotions, or depressed. She needs to get through or let go of what is in the way of her reaching the core of her being.

Nine of Cups

Women have come to the sacred spring of the Poppy Goddess to get water as well as to dance and relax.

UPRIGHT She will get something she's wanted or wished for. Her desires are coming to fruition.

LEFT She's not fully behind what she wants.

RIGHT She's actively seeking or manifesting some wish or desire.

REVERSED She's not trusting her desires, or she does not believe she will get what she's wished for. She may have doubts or lack self-worth.

Ten of Cups

Women give thanks for the rain which will ensure a good harvest.

UPRIGHT She is happy, celebrating and giving thanks for what she has received. She feels an open-hearted fulfillment and a close connection with others.

LEFT She's not fully releasing herself into the love and happiness around her.

RIGHT She's trying to make sure everything goes well.

REVERSED She's having difficulty reaching other people or connecting very deeply in herself. Something feels wrong; she may want to pray, cry for a vision, or call out for help in some way.

Daughter of Cups

The Daughter enjoys a bath in the waterfall while a turtle holds her cup.

UPRIGHT She feels the innocent joy in her body and sexuality as well as the ecstatic pleasure of being in nature's beauty. She is radiating joy to others. She is attractive and charismatic.

LEFT She has low energy and is perhaps inside herself too much.

RIGHT She may have an abundance of play energy or she may try hard to have a good time.

REVERSED She's not open now. She may be unaware of why she's closed. She may feel like she needs a lot and can't get enough, or she may feel lonely, despairing, or overworked.

Son of Cups

A man plays a flute and the seagulls join in his music. The sacred datura plant guides his contemplation.

UPRIGHT He is focused on his creative inner world. He feels a profound sense of calm and peace that makes him an ideal companion and lover. He knows about contemplation and art.

LEFT He is not able to completely focus inside himself. He may be withdrawn but not entirely at peace.

RIGHT He is trying to be true to himself.

REVERSED His access to his intuition or dreams is blocked. He may be dissipating his focus through his ego or talking too much. He needs to take time to relax and feel creative again; he won't do himself or anyone else much good until he draws his energy in and does what he enjoys.

Priestess of Cups

The Priestess, part human and part fish, is joined by a whale and other sea creatures to commune under a full moon.

UPRIGHT She is deeply aware of her inner senses. She may feel very dreamy, sensitive, loving, and open to a very soft and tender place in herself. She feels her personal and collective unconscious as well as the power to merge.

LEFT She is floating without yet being anchored to anything.

RIGHT She feels a pull to go in a particular direction in her inner world. She needs to be sure she wants to go there.

REVERSED She is feeling lost and lonely. Perhaps she is trying to pull people in to take care of her, as there is a tendency to manipulate and feel extremely needy. She's having trouble knowing what to expect from others and what she needs to do herself.

Shaman of Cups

The Shaman wears a mask as she goes about her business mixing and cooking her brew in the cauldron.

UPRIGHT She feels very disciplined and focused on long range goals. There is a real sense of purpose and competency to what she does. Whatever is going on personally she can put aside to meet her responsibilities and be professional.

LEFT She holds back on doing her job or being responsible.

RIGHT She's doing more than her share.

REVERSED She feels inner turbulence or insecurity which she may try to hide from others. She fears losing control or being vulnerable and it's hard for her to express her feelings. Her competency turns to emotional coldness or emotional dramas, crises, or tantrums.

Swords

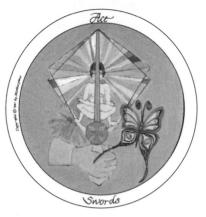

Ace of Swords

A woman balances on a sword as a butterfly guides her vision.

UPRIGHT She takes positive action to achieve a goal. She acts in her best interest by using her will and mental clarity

LEFT She holds back on taking action.

RIGHT She pushes an action or idea.

REVERSED She is involved in negative thoughts or activity. She or someone else is making things go in a bad direction. She could be self-destructive now.

Two of Swords

The stork teaches the woman to balance on one foot while dancing with her swords.

UPRIGHT   She establishes a sense of balance through stillness and not making a decision until she finds her equilibrium. She removes herself from conflict.

LEFT   She's not yet in a state of balance.

RIGHT   She begins to move and be active.

REVERSED   She is ready to engage again after a time out. She may have new insights that support what she chooses to do.

Three of Swords

Three women are challenging each other with their swords.

UPRIGHT She works overtime in her head to control a situation and make sure she comes out on top. There may be a lot of tension or drama now; perhaps she fears losing a lover or some other important partner or project.

LEFT She's not fully engaged in a drama or competitive situation.

RIGHT She's out of control or over her head in some way.

REVERSED There is less intensity in the drama; perhaps she's gaining perspective. She's not taking the "soap opera" antics of a relationship so seriously.

Four of Swords

A woman has placed swords around herself, making a safe space in which to meditate and clear her energy from those around her.

UPRIGHT She removes herself from other people's ideas of what she should do. She puts boundaries around herself to gain some much-needed perspective or space.

LEFT The opinions of others hold more force than her own.

RIGHT She's holding to her own opinions or ideas.

REVERSED Her boundaries are more permeable to new ideas from others. She may be too open and feel overwhelmed, finding it difficult to have time for her own thoughts.

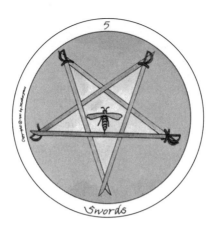

Five of Swords

A yellow jacket has landed, and is surrounded by swords.

UPRIGHT She is in a negative pattern or downward spiral and needs not to panic. Instead she can figure out how the pattern or story is created and look for ways to change it. Much of her energy is drained off into fear of getting stung or wanting to get back at someone.

LEFT She's not completely trapped in the destructive cycle.

RIGHT She uses some control or discipline to change a pattern.

REVERSED She can see a new approach and circumvent a nasty fight or painful sting. She may no longer identify with being the victim or loser.

Six of Swords

A group of women place their swords together and are able to fly.

UPRIGHT She sees clearly what is happening in an all-encompassing way. This allows her to make good but perhaps hard decisions because she understands the consequences and the necessity of her choices.

LEFT She does not see or clearly understand what is happening.

RIGHT She is very sure of her vision and perception.

REVERSED She can't make sense of what she sees or she can't see anything clearly right now. She may feel confused, baffled or bewildered.

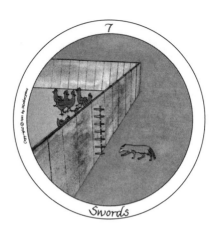

Seven of Swords

A fox figures out a way into the chicken coop.

UPRIGHT She plans or strategizes how to get what she wants. She sees a situation in terms of predator and prey dynamics. She could be acting greedy or stingy.

LEFT She lays back or waits for her strategy to play itself out.

RIGHT She chases something (or someone) down.

REVERSED She no longer needs to plan her every move. She may be able to be more direct and not manipulate. She needs to make amends if she's hurt someone.

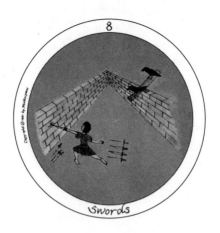

Eight of Swords

A woman breaks her swords against a wall that she invented. The crows are laughing and offering a way out if she would only look around.

UPRIGHT She boxes herself in with a mental picture. The walls she constructed around herself are not real. Perhaps she approaches something too directly or in too linear a way. Maybe she's experiencing recurring anxiety dreams or other very human dilemmas.

LEFT She might experience an unconscious or latent anxiety.

RIGHT She has a tendency to act out a behavior or pattern even though she knows it won't work.

REVERSED She has some perspective on how to let go of anxiety and obsession. She has more of a sense of humor about it all. Perhaps she can see a way around or a way out which will calm her anxiety and make her feel reassured.

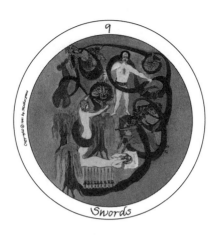

Nine of Swords

A woman has a series of bad dreams and wakes up to face them.

UPRIGHT She experiences fear either through nightmares or negative thoughts. Demons or shadows are active in her psyche or mind. This is a chance for her to know what scares her.

LEFT She may feel vulnerable and have a low capacity for dealing with fear now.

RIGHT She pushes a confrontation with what she fears.

REVERSED She looks at each of the fears one by one in a deep process of turning demons into allies. She understands the positive use of something she has feared inside herself. Power or energy is released because she's no longer controlled by fear.

Ten of Swords

Women leap into the ocean rather then face an army that invaded their sanctuary. The "Thelma and Louise" card.

UPRIGHT She takes a position or fear to its outer limits and there is nowhere else to go with it. She may feel deeply disillusioned, or called to take a very extreme stand or action on a issue that is a basic human right or that is critical to her survival. She jumps into deep emotions.

LEFT She holds back on going off the edge.

RIGHT She goes toward the unknown because she has nothing left to lose.

REVERSED She moves on from what may have been a difficult struggle. She has pushed past her limits and has come through a sacrifice or loss.

Daughter of Swords

The Daughter stands on a rock, waves her sword and whistles for the wind. The wind comes in the shape of a horse and is welcomed by the other inhabitants of the wild land: a mountain goat, black sheep and javelina.

UPRIGHT She has energy to start new things and is ready to stir things up in her life or someone else's. She wants to turn her ideas into something and she doesn't want anything to get in her way.

LEFT She holds back on her power and ability to get things moving.

RIGHT She starts many things at once.

REVERSED She's impatient and frustrated by difficulty. She wants action at any cost and may have attitudes that turn obstacles and delays into anger and defeat.

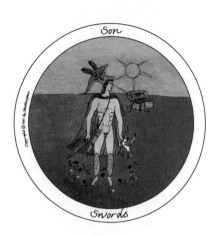

Son of Swords

The Son just won something and is already looking for the next prize. He killed the dove and scattered the roses because he has forgotten to respect life.

UPRIGHT He is set on short-term goals for personal gratification or gain. He is competitive in his means of achieving what he wants. His ideas are disconnected from consequences, and he may show off or insist on getting his way right now.

LEFT He allows other people to influence him.

RIGHT He wants to win at any cost.

REVERSED He's able to take in more than his own agenda. He considers others to be as good as he is. He values art as much as science, or love as much as ideas.

Priestess of Swords

The Priestess climbs to a mountain top to send off her wishes and prayers with a snowy owl on the night of a full moon.

UPRIGHT She's clear about her purpose and direction. She can go off by herself and still stay responsible and connected to others. She has integrity by knowing how to have joy and discipline in her life. She sends out her wishes or desires.

LEFT She doesn't trust herself.

RIGHT She's very sure of herself.

REVERSED Her clear mind is twisted in on itself, becoming judgmental and full of criticism. She may feel lonely, depressed, withdrawn, or cold, and may feel like someone else is at fault. Or she may feel herself deeply and mysteriously to blame. It is time to realize that not everything will end badly and to learn to find love where it is available.

Shaman of Swords

The Shaman blows a wind from her mind and heart that travels up the spirit ladder to receive a message from the swallow-tailed kite.

UPRIGHT She's able to speak directly and truthfully about her values and desires. What she says is consistent and comes from her heart. She has clear insights which result in respect and cooperation from others.

LEFT She holds back on what she knows to be true.

RIGHT She speaks out with great authority or conviction.

REVERSED She's not able to say what she sees and feels. Perhaps she doesn't want to stir up someone's anger or risk a relationship ending. She will continue to be subject to someone else's domination if she doesn't take the initiative wherever she can and communicate what she knows to be true.

Discs

Ace of Discs

After playing a game with acorns, a baby naps by a fire while a leopard cub licks her stomach.

UPRIGHT She creates something or receives a gift. She has a sense of well-being, safety, security, and comfort.

LEFT She hesitates about receiving something that is presented to her.

RIGHT She goes out to meet what's coming her way.

REVERSED She may not want what she is now offered. She may reconsider something that she thought she wanted. There might be obstacles, or an impasse, to something she thought she would get.

Two of Discs

A woman nurses twin babies as she is held in a circle by a double-headed snake.

UPRIGHT She is able to handle a lot now and there is a great variety of things she does or roles she plays. She can meet many diverse needs.

LEFT She isn't fully available to everything that pulls on her.

RIGHT She's handling more than her share.

REVERSED She doesn't want to have a very complicated life now. She wants simplicity and finds it hard to juggle two or more responsibilities, obligations or activities in her life. She may want space or freedom from responsibility now.

Three of Discs

The women are building a house together.

UPRIGHT She's devoted to her work and others are willing to help her or give her recognition and money. There is purpose and meaning in what she is doing.

LEFT She is distracted or held back from her work.

RIGHT She's working hard and putting forth effort to achieve an end.

REVERSED She's not satisfied with her work. Perhaps she doesn't have the money or recognition she's been seeking and there may be problems working with others or getting cooperation.

Four of Discs

A woman stands at her doorway ready to open or close the door. Behind her a rock deflects the wind from the fire.

UPRIGHT She controls who comes in and who stays out and when. She needs peaceful time and nurturing space to be with herself. Perhaps she needs space to be creative.

LEFT She is unable to fully shut out all that presses in on her.

RIGHT She pushes out whatever is extraneous to what she wants to do.

REVERSED It may be hard to say no as she is over run by people and things. Perhaps she is choosing to be open to an influx of activity.

Five of Discs

A woman kneads dough to make bread.

UPRIGHT She is in a waiting time and there may be a tendency to worry. She can do simple, basic tasks to ground and calm herself. She may be feeling stress about survival, money issues or not having enough of something.

LEFT She may not have much strength now to do even simple tasks, and she needs to go slowly.

RIGHT She directs her worry into activity.

REVERSED She isn't consumed by the obstacles in her life. She creates alternatives and other options for herself. She's discovered new ways of taking care of herself.

Six of Discs

A woman massages and heals another.

UPRIGHT She is able to give and take easily and has enough to share. She can be generous now and is open to healing.

LEFT She may not see an outlet for what she has to give.

RIGHT She may give more than she receives.

REVERSED She does not want to give out any personal energy or information about herself. She's cutting herself off from others. She may fear success or deeply connecting or committing herself to someone.

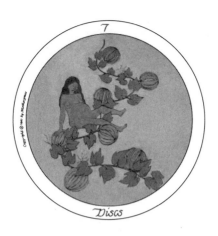

Seven of Discs

A woman is pregnant and waiting for her baby to be born and the melons to ripen.

UPRIGHT She waits for something to be born and is in a period of gestation or incubating. She is in the last part of inner growth before the harvest, birth, or end product.

LEFT She inhibits or slows down the gestation.

RIGHT She pushes the birth.

REVERSED She is impatient or even anxious to be done with waiting. She wants whatever it is to hurry up and manifest. She may even be obsessively watching herself and her process. She needs to trust the time it takes for what she wants to happen.

Eight of Discs

A group of women gathers to share their work.

UPRIGHT She finds deep meaning in her daily life because there is purpose and connection to others in her work. She may feel like she's always developing her craft, even though she has already mastered many skills.

LEFT She's not so sure of what she's doing.

RIGHT She's very confident about what she's doing. Perhaps she leads or teaches.

REVERSED She's uninspired about her life, particularly her work. There seems to be no meaning or camaraderie in what she does. She may be underutilized or bored, or she may desire a change of career.

Nine of Discs

A healer woman has come to the desert to create a sand painting.

UPRIGHT She is in a solitary and creative period. She is connected to her healing and artistic abilities and may want to be outside around more of the non-human creatures.

LEFT She isn't fully engaged in her artistic healing nature.

RIGHT She's very busy with her creative energy.

REVERSED She can't be alone and it may be a time to go out with what she's done while she was alone. Or she may not be able to get anything done because of a lack of self-motivation, a fear of working alone or just not being able to get any space to do anything.

Ten of Discs

The women of the community gather to welcome new life as a mother has a baby.

UPRIGHT She gives birth actually or metaphorically with community support and sanction. Whatever she brings forth is welcomed by those around her. She produces with ease.

LEFT She hesitates in coming out with something. Or the support around her isn't fully available.

RIGHT She and her community are actively pushing something out in the world.

REVERSED She has a difficult time bringing something out; it is a breech or hard birth. Perhaps she feels family pressures or a lack of community support and may not have much to show for a great deal of work.

Daughter of Discs

The Daughter stands in a place of power by the *sipápuni* (Hopi word) or birth hole. She rests her medicine pipe in the sacred circle. Behind her is her house in a cave. The sun has set, and the full moon rises and reflects in her obsidian mirror.

UPRIGHT She's open and receptive as well as courageous and determined. She's willing to wait for the inspiration and information she needs to go forward in her life. She seeks a kind of knowledge that is based in the truth that comes through her body.

LEFT She may feel doubt about being open to new inspiration.

RIGHT She's eager to explore new territory in her body or outside herself.

REVERSED She may feel small and insecure or aware of how she's been teased or misunderstood in the past. She may need to seek a vision or new source of strength inside herself. It is through the process of falling down and getting up again that certain truth and instinctual wisdom are cultivated. She learns how to handle suffering, although she does not seek it.

Son of Discs

The Son is an elf in the woods with an English robin and a dragonfly. They focus on hitting the center of the target.

UPRIGHT He knows what he wants and is willing to work for it. He focuses on specific goals in a meticulous, grounded, confident, and fair way.

LEFT He lacks some follow-through to achieve his goals.

RIGHT He works overtime to accomplish something.

REVERSED He may have given up before trying; perhaps he doesn't know what to aim at. He doesn't have the inner confidence or trust to really focus on what he wants, and cannot use his ability to accomplish his goals.

Priestess of Discs

The Priestess is doing yoga and other inner work to care for herself as the parrot takes care of her baby.

UPRIGHT She is very aware of what her body needs. She takes care of herself and can also nurture and give pleasure to others if she wants to.

LEFT She's vague about what her body wants and she needs to sharpen her senses.

RIGHT She works to maintain or heal her own or someone else's body.

REVERSED She's not feeling well. Perhaps she doesn't know what she needs or is not aware of her body. It is not a time to try to take care of others, since she is the one who needs attention.

Shaman of Discs

The Shaman rides her donkey to the people who need her healing, and on the way holds council with the bald eagle.

UPRIGHT She knows where she's going. She has long range visions and goals. She knows how to be connected to life-long relationships, and how to go about her work alone if necessary.

LEFT She's not so sure about where she's going.

RIGHT She follows a strong pull in a particular direction. She needs to be sure not to neglect other parts of her life for too long.

REVERSED She doesn't feel in contact with the life that is opening up ahead of her. Her life seems to have come to a halt, or is over in some way. She lacks foresight, and perhaps needs to take a risk or do something to remind herself of her inherent wisdom and abilities. There may be a new skill she needs to acquire before she can move forward again.

Bibliography

I'm grateful to the many fine scholars, artists, teachers, healers and priestesses whose books directly and indirectly influenced my understanding of the Goddess and the tarot. I appreciate the wide range of perspectives and traditions that are represented by the work of these authors. I'm very fortunate to have their brilliant books in my life.

Allione, Tsultrim. *Women of Wisdom*. Routledge and Kegan Paul, 1984.

Austen, Hallie Iglehart. *The Heart of the Goddess*. Wingbow, 1990.

Awiakta, Marilou. *Selu: Seeking the Corn-Mother's Wisdom*. Fulcrum, 1993.

Bolen, Jean Shinoda. *Goddesses in Every Woman: A New Psychology of Women*. Harper & Row, 1984.

Budapest, Z. *The Holy Book of Women's Mysteries*. Wingbow, 1980.

Dorkenoo, Efua. *Cutting the Rose: Female Genital Mutilation: The Practice and its Prevention*. Minority Rights Group, 1994.

Eisler, Riane. *The Chalice and the Blade*. Harper and Row, 1987.

Gadon, Elinor. *The Once and Future Goddess: A Symbol for Our Time*. Harper & Row, 1989.

Gimbutas, Marija. *The Language of the Goddess*. HarperSanFrancisco, 1989.

Gimbutas, Marija. *The Civilization of the Goddess*. HarperSanFrancisco, 1991.

Griffin, Susan. *Woman and Nature: The Roaring Inside Her*. Harper & Row, 1979.

Lerner, Gerder. *The Creation of Patriarchy*. Oxford University Press, 1986.

Mariechild, Diane. *Mother Wit: A Feminist Guide to Psychic Development*. Crossing Press, 1981.

Noble, Vicki. *Motherpeace: A Way to the Goddess through Myth, Art, and Tarot*. HarperSanFrancisco, 1983.

Noble, Vicki and Jonathan Tenney. *The Motherpeace Playbook*. Wingbow Press, 1986.

Noble, Vicki. *Shakti Woman*. HarperSanFrancisco, 1991.

Oda, Mayumi. *Goddesses*. Volcano Press, 1981.

Sjöö, Monica, and Barbara Mor. *The Great Cosmic Mother*. Harper & Row, 1987.

Spretnak, Charlene. *Lost Goddesses of Early Greece: A Collection of Pre-Hellenic Mythology*. Beacon Press, 1978.

Starhawk. *The Spiral Dance*. Harper & Row, 1979.

Stone, Merlin. *When God Was a Woman*. Harcourt Brace Jovanovich, 1976.

Tanner, Nancy Makepeace. *On Becoming Human*. Cambridge University Press, 1981.

Tanner, Nancy M., and Adrienne L. Zihlman. "Women in Evolution 1. Innovation and Selection in Human Origins." *Signs: Journal of Women in Culture and Society*, 1:585-608, 1976.

Teish, Luisah. *Jambalaya: The Natural Woman's Book of Personal Charms*. Harper and Row, 1985.

Von Wuthenau, Alexander. *The Art of Terracotta Pottery in Pre-Columbian Central and South America*. Crown Publishing, 1969.

Walker, Alice. *Temple of My Familiar*. Harcourt Brace Jovanovich, 1989.

Walker, Barbara G. *Women's Encyclopedia of Myths and Secrets*. Harper & Row, 1988.

Wynne, Patrice. *The Womanspirit Sourcebook*. Harper & Row, 1988.

Photograph by Nonnie Welch

Karen Vogel is an artist, teacher and the co-creator of the Motherpeace Tarot deck. Her artwork includes wood sculpture, dolls, beadwork, stained glass, and furniture. She lives in Point Reyes, California.